COLOURS ON MY FACE

Palmwine Publishing

By Itohan Ekle

Copyright © Itohan Ekle

All rights reserved. No part of this publication may be reproduced, distributed, or transmitted in any form or by any means, including photocopying, recording, or other electronic or mechanical methods, without the prior written permission of the publisher, except in the case of brief quotations embodied in critical reviews and certain other non-commercial uses permitted by copyright law.

Author- Itohan Ekle

ISBN-(Paperback)-978-1-917267-35-9

ISBN (E-Book)- 978-1-917267-36-6

Published by Nubian Republic on behalf of Palmwine Publishing Limited Nigeria

Email: info@palmwinepublishing.com

Address- UK: 86-90, Paul Street, London EC2A 4NE

Address-Nigeria: 1A Jos Road Bukuru, Plateau State, Nigeria.
www.palmwinepublishing.com
www.raffiapress.com
www.nuciferaanalysis.com

Table of Contents

Le Pills Du Truth --------------------------------- 3
Sunflower Look-Alikes ---------------------------- 7
A Bullet or A Word-------------------------------- 11
Gain From the Pain-------------------------------- 14
Dear Moon--- 17
Dear Mother Earth--------------------------------- 21
Two Little Kids----------------------------------- 28
Mountain of Nudity-------------------------------- 32
Be Strong--- 36
I Am Going To War With Myself--------------------- 40
Your Grown Daughter------------------------------- 45
I Will Sing Along--------------------------------- 50
Dear African Child-------------------------------- 53
Vienna (City Of Dreams)--------------------------- 59
Earth Is Your Place------------------------------- 61
Yes, I Am A Woman--------------------------------- 64
Lava Is On Today's Menu--------------------------- 70
In-house Gas-------------------------------------- 74
Do You See Her------------------------------------ 78
Tales of Despair---------------------------------- 83
About The Author---------------------------------- 87

Colours On My Face by Itohan Ekle

LE PILLS DU TRUTH

"I have never seen this type of cancer before," the doctor exclaimed.
"What is it called?" the patient asked.
"I don't know; I have to consult with the headquarters."

At the headquarters—
"What is the name?" the doctor asked the director.
"It is called cancer of the lies."
"How is this possible?"

Colours On My Face by Itohan Ekle

"It is caused by lying to yourself often."
"Is it lethal?"
"Yes. I have seen many cases like this; only a few have survived.
It is in stage 10."
"Stage 10?" the doctor asked, surprised.
"Yes."

"Is there a cure?"
"Yes, but it is still in the labs. However, your patient can try it."

"What is this?"
"It is called Le Pills du Truth, also known as the Truth Tablet."
"What is the prescription?"
"Thrice a day, preferably after every meal."

"Has this ever cured anyone?"
"Well, your patient will have to try and see."

"I have to attend to another patient with
Blindly Loving.
We are still trying to manufacture a drug for that."

"Tell your patient to swallow the pills with lemon juice,
in the bathroom,
All alone,

Close to a sink."

"Well, people who have used this treatment said they threw up or purged the cancer out of their system."
"That means it works?" the doctor asked.
"Some people didn't finish it, and for others, the cancer had already progressed too much.
Also, it is a lifetime treatment," the director replied.

"Tell your patient they can start
The treatment at their earliest convenience."

The nurse enters.
"We have another case.
The patient just came in unconscious.
It looks like
Misplaced Priorities."

"Misplaced Priorities?
Very few survive this.
Take the patient to the ICU and get me Doctor A Slap of Reality."

"Doctor, wait.
Can she come in for chemo?"
"The pill is the chemo.
Remember, three pills of the Truth Tablet,
Three times a day."

"Yes," the doctor nods while jotting.
"With lemon juice, in the bathroom."

"Thanks, Director.
Very few hospitals give
Intensive treatment like this."
"That's why we are the headquarters."

"Now I must go.
Scurry along,
Doctor Common Sense."
"Bye,
Specialist Back to Earth," The director replied.

SUNFLOWER LOOK-ALIKES

You look like a sunflower, But
you are not. You are all packed
so closely.

Colours On My Face by Itohan Ekle

When I first saw you,

I thought you were a sunflower.

You stood on bare land,

Opposite a huge school.

Every Sunday after church,

I would pass by you,

And I would stare at you,

Soaking in your beauty.

I would look at the empty land

That was once a big market,

Now occupied by you.

You were never planted by anyone.

You are, and will always be,

A beautiful weed.

I imagined you all were a family—
Individual plants that came
Together to form a little garden. You
lightened up my day. Seeing you
every Sunday Was the best part of
my day.

You grew on bare land
Where a huge market once stood,
Years ago, demolished
By the government.

You are a mirror
Into my own life—
A beacon of hope.
You represent tranquillity.
You remind me that
My life, once rich and

Colours On My Face by Itohan Ekle

Bustling, but demolished by loss,

Can still produce Something as

beautiful As you.

Colours On My Face by Itohan Ekle

A BULLET OR A WORD

Talking is the easy part.

Thinking adequately

and observing with an open mind—

that is the real challenge,

which is why some people

choose to avoid it.

Colours On My Face by Itohan Ekle

I used to let your words

bore holes so deep in me

that they pierced through

the other side of my chest.

But now, I've learned to dodge

your bullets in the form of advice

and seemingly well-meaning words.

Now, I carry a scalpel,

removing each bullet

you lodged in me.

The operation is excruciating—

tearing into bleeding flesh hurts—

but I will persist,

removing every single one,

no matter how long it takes.

Colours On My Face by Itohan Ekle

I was already broken

when you started firing,

but you didn't have to shatter me.

The holes you created—

I promise to fill them,

so completely

you won't even notice

there was ever an abyss.

And the next time I see you,

I'll be wearing

a bulletproof vest.

GAIN FROM THE PAIN

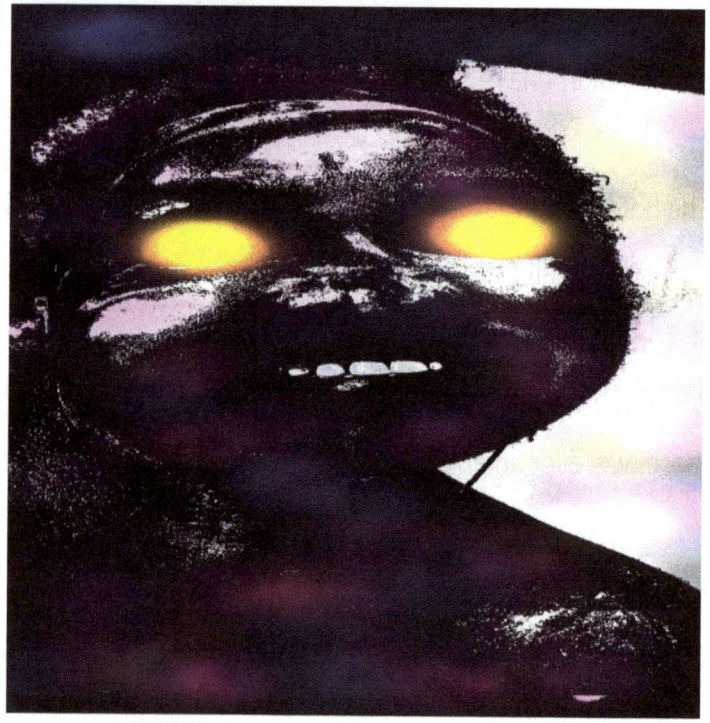

Even if it feels like rain,

Some of it still is pain.

I'm just trying to make some gains,

Even if I am losing again,

Just letting the hurt feign.

Colours On My Face by Itohan Ekle

It was too sweet to end in pain;

I am trying to separate the pain from the gain.

So let me bargain,

Because my heart is too slain

To seek you again.

The good memories I will maintain;

My full potential I will attain.

But the scars don't make it feel like a complete gain,

Even if the passion subdues the pain.

I know it will rise again,

And in the same vein,

Take all my gains

And leave me with pain.

Colours On My Face by Itohan Ekle

But I will also rise again

And not be vain.

I will cherish my gains

And shield them from the pain,

And with all my heart, maintain.

I will shut out the reign

Of misplaced priorities like a drain

And enjoy every moment like a grain.

In me, an open heart I will engrain.

The fire in me, no cage can contain.

My mental health I shall regain,

So that I might one day full happiness attain.

DEAR MOON

Dear Moon, you need no introduction

Or invitation to my events.

You were there the day I was born,

You watched me grow.

You studied me—my habits, my grief,

Colours On My Face by Itohan Ekle

My happiness, and my activities.

I turned and turned in bed tonight
But was unable to sleep.
I took our conversation piece and
Went out the back door.
There you were, waiting for me as always.

I was happy that even in my darkest moment,
You shone brighter than the dark clouds
That covered my heart.

Funny enough,
You are one of the few
That is always there, does not judge me,
And does not play my mistakes
Like a song that never ends.
I met you when I was a little girl.

Colours On My Face by Itohan Ekle

You were far older than me, but

Age is just a number when it comes to us.

I could only play with you freely

When I was at my grandparent's apartment.

We have a common enemy

Called the sun.

It drives you away from me

Because it is bigger

And pours its heat on me.

But in the night,

You cool me off from the sun's terrors.

You have shown me things

Words can't express.

I promise, when it's only just the two of us,

I will spend my whole night with you.

Colours On My Face by Itohan Ekle

I know when I am buried,

You will visit my grave

Till the day you die as well.

Dear Moon, please don't grow old,

Because the more we age

The more we lose ourselves.

Colours On My Face by Itohan Ekle

DEAR MOTHER EARTH

Dear Mother Earth,

Colours On My Face by Itohan Ekle

You have formed us from yourself.

We are a reflection of you;

Your diversity is seen

In how unique we all are.

I have lived with an observant eye.

I am in awe of your beauty,

Amazed by your wonders,

And broken by your wars and ignorance.

Dear Mother Earth,

You have given us so much.

Why can't we build

Rather than destroy?

Why can't we trade pride and culture

For peace and progress?

Why can't we make you more beautiful

Through our actions?

Colours On My Face by Itohan Ekle

We are a piece in your puzzle.

Can't we learn to see ourselves

In this light?

Instead of seeing one another

As mortal enemies,

Why can't we see ourselves

As worthy companions and competitors?

Instead of moulding each other

To fit our desires,

Can't we look beyond ourselves—

One piece in the bigger puzzle?

Dear Earth, you have gifted us

With countless species.

Why can't we value them,

Rather than see our differences

Colours On My Face by Itohan Ekle

As our weaknesses?

We are you.

By building you,

We build ourselves.

By hurting you,

We destroy ourselves.

Dear Earth, why do we teach

Our sons to focus only on

The size of their fists, balls, and wallets,

The depth of their voices,

And how "manly" they appear?

Why don't we teach them

That true value lies

In a well-developed mind,

In strength that embraces

Both vulnerability and power?

True power isn't denying weakness
Or hiding behind bold words.
True power is accepting
Frailties, highs, and lows.

We rob men of the privilege
To truly feel—
To express emotions
That society claims belong
Only to women.

Just because we deny it
Doesn't mean it isn't there,
Piling up and waiting to erupt.

Dear Mother Earth,

Colours On My Face by Itohan Ekle

Why do we teach our daughters

To focus on their curves and ass—

On how sexy and attractive

They can be to a man?

Why don't we tell them

These things are nothing in comparison

To a woman who sees herself

Beyond society's labels—

A woman who recognizes

Her potential, possibilities,

And the vastness of a free,

Well-developed mind?

Why does the media claim

To empower women

While reducing them

To mere sex objects?

This isn't empowerment—

It's demeaning and destructive.

Dear Mother Earth,

I hope we can trade the trivial

For the urgent.

Let intellect lead before ego,

Prioritize our collective needs over individual wants.

I truly hope we can learn

To see ourselves as humans first—

Before anything else.

Colours On My Face by Itohan Ekle

TWO LITTLE KIDS

Colours On My Face by Itohan Ekle

It was a few days before Christmas,

Two kids lying side by side on the floor in the living room,

Screaming with excitement at the sound of fireworks.

"Keep quiet! If we are told to run, we won't hear,"

Their mother silenced them.

She succeeded in quieting their voices

But could not silence their excitement and imagination.

They became inspired to create what they had never seen—

Just two little kids who had only heard the sound of fireworks.

They made their way to the master bedroom,

With a matchbox in their hands and hearts full of optimism.

They struck a matchstick on the large wooden table filled with books,

Waiting for fireworks to appear.

Colours On My Face by Itohan Ekle

Disappointed when none came,

They returned to the living room.

A few moments later,

Smoke quickly filled the air, as wood and fire are not good friends in a home.

Documents and clothes burned as the curtains and bed

Were moments away from catching fire.

A harmless adventure quickly turned into

Neighbours frantically trying to quench the flames.

The two kids stood in awe as smoke billowed from their house,

Watching people run with buckets of water.

In the end, no fireworks were created.

The only good thing to come of it

Was the long-overdue home renovation.

Colours On My Face by Itohan Ekle

Maybe we all need a little fire to renovate our lives,

And the little kids in us are perfect for the job.

It won't create fireworks that last only a brief moment,

But it will leave a memory that lasts a lifetime—

And probably generations,

If you're a good storyteller.

Colours On My Face by Itohan Ekle

THE MOUNTAIN OF NUDITY

Colours On My Face by Itohan Ekle

There is a mountain above the stars,

Not made of sand, rocks, or stones—

A mountain of clouds, bigger than the earth,

But one that can only accommodate one at a time.

The stars try to get close but are unable to;

The moon visits often.

It has the aura of tranquillity.

There, you can come as you are;

You can even come naked, and no cops will arrest you.

Well, not the nakedness of clothes, but of the mind.

It is where you drop everything for the first time—

Your knowledge, your pride, your strengths—and embrace nudity in its most extreme form.

Colours On My Face by Itohan Ekle

It is where you decide to take a long-overdue, deep breath before you lose your mind.

It is a place where robes are illegal—

Where robes of fear and having our guards up are removed,

And you are just there, naked

To our deepest hurts, weaknesses, and loss.

You can cry, laugh, meditate, or do all at the same time.

You can be authentically yourself and

Spare yourself from all life's bullshit for the first time.

In this mountain, there is no

Disapproving stare of people who misunderstand you.

You can be the craziest version of yourself.

I visit this mountain often;

I prefer going at midnight when I hear no voice and see no face.

Colours On My Face by Itohan Ekle

This is the peak of my nudity.

This is where I imagine myself naked while

All my suppressed emotions stare at me.

So I say, you can take off your clothes, but you don't want to go "nude" with me.

Colours On My Face by Itohan Ekle

BE STRONG

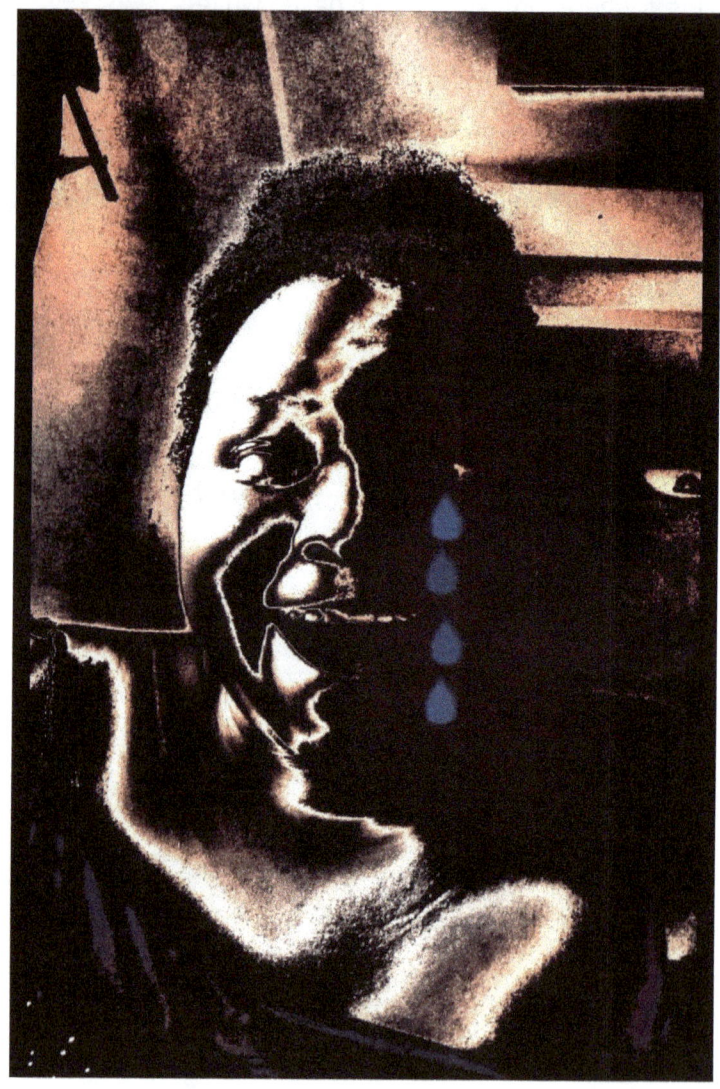

Be strong.

Two words oblivious to the reality of hurt and clinical depression.

Telling someone who is hurt to be strong is like telling a sick person to be healthy.

Two words that wreak so much damage,

Two words that have created a deadly cycle.

They show how the speaker is not in touch with reality and tell the listener, "You are going to have to go through this all alone."

But what if, in that situation, "to be strong" is not a possibility?

What if, in that situation, to be broken is all the person knows and the only language the person speaks?

What if it is just "to be weak"?

But I have come to understand what "to be strong" means.

It sometimes means acting like you are okay when inside you are indeed dying.

It means trivializing and demeaning the pain.

I have grown tired of being strong.

It was all I ever did.

It was all I was taught as a child.

I did it to the extent that I didn't realize I was depressed as a child.

But those two words, "be strong," cause damage; they are a lethal poison.
It is to pile pain upon pain without dealing with it and pretend it is not there until it becomes an ocean that sweeps and drowns you in it.

Maybe, if we are "weak,"

We will be able to deal with the pain one at a time and not pile it up.

Maybe, if we are "weak,"

We will have the resources to cope with emotional trauma and not treat it like an alien invasion.

Maybe, if we are "weak,"

We will be able to save more lives and prevent more people from committing suicide.

Real strength is in acceptance, not denial.

When we deny, we subconsciously tell our brains it is too powerful for us to handle.

Colours On My Face by Itohan Ekle

I AM GOING TO WAR WITH MYSELF

Colours On My Face by Itohan Ekle

Dear Me,

We must fight

This night.

You have taken the light

And left me with fright.

But I am bright,

And my sight

Will be my plight.

I won't let you take flight.

Dear Me,

I have had enough of you.

You have lied to me,

And I have believed your lies

Since I was a child.

You made me think you were

Small.

Colours On My Face by Itohan Ekle

You have traded your worth for belonging.

Dear Me,

I am angry at you.

Sometimes, I despise you for not

Being brave enough to end toxic relationships.

I am unhappy that you are happy in public,

But you cry in the shower so you can't

Differentiate between your tears

And the water from the shower.

Dear Me,

I am unhappy that you were

Too late to start

Learning how to love yourself.

I am saddened that you wanted people to accept you

Colours On My Face by Itohan Ekle

When you did not accept yourself first.

Dear Me,

I don't want you to think I have written you off.

Although you offend me often,

The fact that you let people write you off,

And you accepted it—

That, I can't forgive you for.

Dear Me,

Don't confuse my rebuke for hatred.

And don't think me talking to myself is madness.

It is proof of my tiredness

At how you decided to be naive in the face of truth.

Dear Me,

I love you,

But I want you to love us more now,

Colours On My Face by Itohan Ekle

More than being oblivious.

Dear Me,

Don't take this personally.

I am just going to war with myself.

We shall rumble,

Because we both have stumbled.

But now is not the time to fumble.

Do not grumble.

I shall crumble

All that holds you in a bubble.

May the best me win.

Colours On My Face by Itohan Ekle

YOUR GROWN DAUGHTER

The joy of knowing I didn't lose you—

The solace of knowing it could have been so much worse.

The pain you carried,

The self-hatred that consumed you,

Colours On My Face by Itohan Ekle

I felt it.

The feeling of helplessness,

Hopelessness, and despair

You tried to cover with your jokes,

I felt that so painfully

When I saw you on the

Hospital bed in Maitama.

I saw how frustration and disappointment

Seeped into your body,

Weighing you down.

And yet, through the hurt,

You did everything to shield me.

You always made sure there was food on the table,

Clothes on my back, shoes on my feet.

You gave love,

Even when it meant sacrificing your own needs and reputation.

Colours On My Face by Itohan Ekle

I remember you standing tall,

When someone wanted to harass me,

You were not going to have any of it.

You fought to protect me,

Even if it meant putting

Yourself through the fire.

Now, I wish I could go back—

To be the little girl holding your hand,

Sitting close to you in church,

Running to you for comfort.

I wish I could relive the days

When you wrapped wedding gifts on Saturdays; our duo weekend out,

Or let me model Kampala gowns for your customers.

Colours On My Face by Itohan Ekle

I wish I could sleep beside you

On nights I have nightmares about horror movies I watched during the day.

I wish we could go back to our kitchen in Kubwa when I was learning how to cook Jollof rice and it always ended undercooked or overcooked.

But,

Now, I need to be your grown daughter.

I want to release you from your guilt,

The guilt that whispers you didn't do enough,

The pain that convinces you of failure.

You gave everything,

And I see that now.

Colours On My Face by Itohan Ekle

I want to hold your hands,

Like you once held mine when I was a child.

I want to look into your eyes and tell you,

"It's going to be okay,"

Not just to comfort you,

But because I truly believe it will.

I want to shield you from hurt,

The way you shielded me.

But how can I protect you,

When I can't even protect myself?

I want to make you laugh,

Not just at my silly jokes,

But because you finally feel peace—

Peace in knowing the storm is over.

I WILL SING ALONG

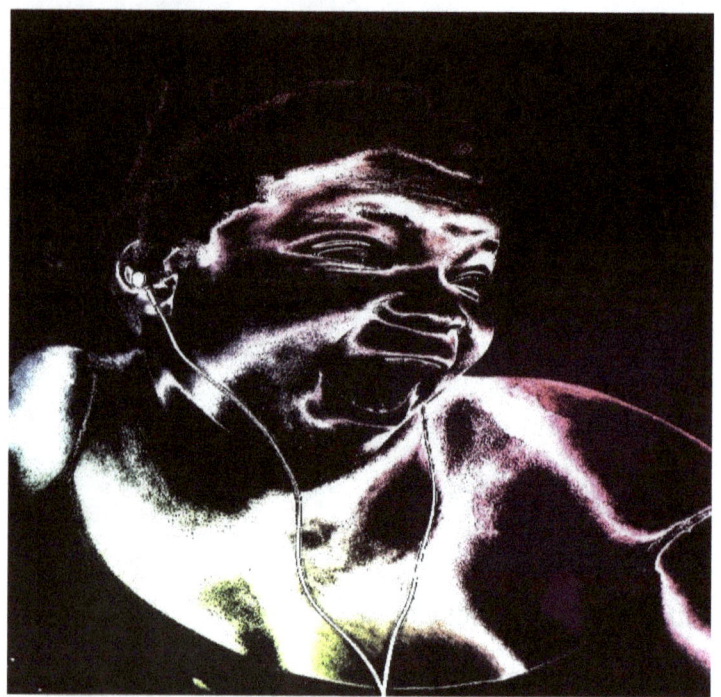

Sing it like a love song. You know I will sing along. Don't be terrified; it's only pain in my voice.

Even though you sing it to hurt me and break me, I will still sing along.

Don't be terrified; I will be terrified for me.

Colours On My Face by Itohan Ekle

Sing it with all your heart,

Even though you ripped out mine.

I will still sing with an open heart—literally.

Don't be terrified.

It is only pain in my voice.

Sometimes, when I look up to the sky, I see only the moon despite the uncountable stars above. I see only a dead, lonely planet up there without oxygen. The moon gives me peace and reminds me of myself.

It is only pain in my voice, nothing more.

Not love. Not hate. Not hope. Not dreams. Not aspirations.

Just pain.

Colours On My Face by Itohan Ekle

Please, sing it like a love song, even though it is meant to break me.

I promise I will sing along.

But don't be terrified;

It's only pain inside my voice.

Colours On My Face by Itohan Ekle

DEAR AFRICAN CHILD

Dear African child, I see you coming from a distance.

Your swollen leg is not as heavy as your heart.

Only you know your pain,

Only you know your shame,

Only you know your stains.

Colours On My Face by Itohan Ekle

Dear African child, let the mockers mock;

Let the scorners scorn.

Although you wear rags and your shoes are worn out,

You will wear golden shoes.

You will wear clean clothes.

Yesterday was not yours;

Today does not belong to you;

Tomorrow is yours.

Dear African child, don't let your swollen face define your beauty—
It lies inwardly, not outwardly.

Only you know your true scars.

You are a work in progress;

Your power is not in today but in tomorrow.

You alone know your shame;

You alone will know your glory.

Colours On My Face by Itohan Ekle

The world calls you unfortunate, unlucky,

But only you know your story.

You are as your landscape—dogged, unyielding,

You are like a tree trying to take root in a desert.

Only you know your struggles.

Your face tells stories of years of intimidation and fear,

Of disunity and conflict,

Of genocide and hypocrisy.

Your face also tells stories of hopelessness and faith,

Of fear and courage,

Of killings and activism,

Of hunger and generosity,

Of corruption and honesty.

Colours On My Face by Itohan Ekle

Your heart panics not just for the present but for the future.

You are tired of being an object of pity, scorn, labels.

You are tired of being labelled entirely as a scammer because of where you are from.
Your heart aches when people ask where you're from,

Because you know their guard will go up due to your nationality.

You want to be seen beyond a philanthropic action, an SOS call to the rest of the world.
You want to be seen beyond just an immigrant, or an illegal immigrant.
You want to be seen beyond a third-world nation.

You want to go out and vote without fear that you will never return home.
You need to know your vote counts.

Deep down, above the pity and scorn,

You want to be seen for your dreams, potentials, possibilities.
You want to be seen for the power of your mind.

Colours On My Face by Itohan Ekle

You are just barely holding on to life,

Trying to be someone when everything pushes you to the ground.

I mean, literally everything.

At home, you are not really at home.

Abroad, you do not find peace and live in constant fear.

As much as you appreciate well-meaning foreign attention,
You don't want the kind of foreign attention that dwells only on the negatives.
Deep down, you don't want that to be your only story.

Deep down, you just want a little bit of something positive for once,

To be associated with something good.

Deep down, you just want to be humanized—

Maybe just once.

Only you know your mind.

Dear African child,

Don't forget,

Tomorrow belongs to you.

Colours On My Face by Itohan Ekle

VIENNA (City of Dreams)

It was like running a race, almost tasting the sky,

When suddenly your leg twists, and you fall,

Rolling in pain as the finish line fades.

It was like studying all night for a test,

Answering every question confidently,

Only to watch the papers burn

And be given a new test on a different subject.

Colours On My Face by Itohan Ekle

It was like preparing a perfect meal,
Rehearsing every detail for the competition,
Only to get stuck in traffic, arriving too late to compete.

It was also like believing you had the solution,
But only making things worse—
Like a million déjà vu in a single year.

Now, it's the little needles that pierce your heart—
Not even the tides changing to mark another failed attempt,
But the ache of belonging to nothing
That was once everything.

Colours On My Face by Itohan Ekle

EARTH IS YOUR PLACE

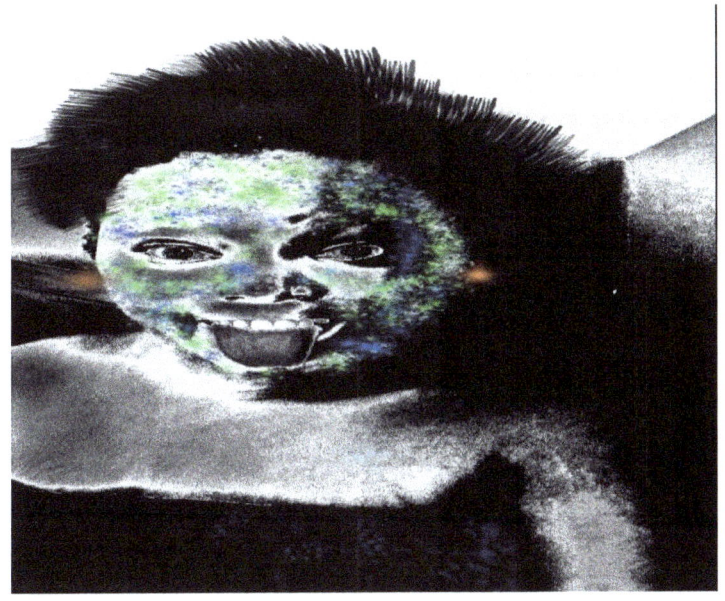

Even if you fail,

Stay on the trail.

Do not derail;

Accept you might be frail.

Don't bail—

With your tail,

You shall one day prevail,

Although now you travail.

Colours On My Face by Itohan Ekle

When you are in a fight,

You may lose your might,

But don't alight.

The future is bright;

Cling to any light,

Even though it feels like an unending night—

The journey is the delight.

So what if you lose a fight?

You can slow your pace,

Give yourself some space.

Put on your determined face;

Wear your hopes like lace.

Don't let anything displace

You from your race.

Life indeed is a maze.

A way out you will learn to trace.

Pursue your dream with grace—

Earth is your place.

Colours On My Face by Itohan Ekle

YES, I AM A WOMAN

Yes, I am a woman,

But I am also human.

Yes, I am a woman,

But I possess a free mind.

Colours On My Face by Itohan Ekle

I am a true one, With stories of
perseverance That have stretched
across generations.

I might be a woman,
But I won't be society's crude
To refine and sell however they deem fit.

I won't accept the sexist slur,
"Shake for the dollar," as a compliment
or as "empowerment."

I am a woman, yes, but I will brood
Over every storm life throws my way.
I shall not accept any labels,
Because I have a free mind,
From a free kind.

Colours On My Face by Itohan Ekle

Many women have sacrificed everything,

For someone like me to even

Be able to choose.

I will also sacrifice everything one day,

So that generations to come

Will only hear there was once

Something called gender inequality,

But it will not be their reality.

My mother always says I look like

Her grandmother, who lived beyond 100.

I am, indeed, a reflection of my feminine ancestors.

In my former life, I was a warrior.

I am a woman.

I will resist any intruder

Trying to define me

Irregularly.

I am a woman,

But I am not a

Second-class human.

I am a woman,

And I am proud

Of who I am.

I am a woman,

I am a free tribe,

Not to be confused

With a caged type.

I am a raised kind,

From lies that

Went down centuries ago.

Colours On My Face by Itohan Ekle

I am a woman,

And I am a schooled type—

Schooled in wisdom beyond academics,

Beyond norms.

I will not confuse the "b" word as entertainment,

Nor applaud it.

I am a woman,

And I am a cruiser,

Not to be chained to one

Thing and one thing alone.

I am a woman,

And I love me.

This is my humanity.

Colours On My Face by Itohan Ekle

Despite the sexist stereotypes,

I am proud of being a true one.

My struggles have built me up,

Connecting me to years of fight.

I am a woman,

And I am a fighter.

I wouldn't have me any other way.

Colours On My Face by Itohan Ekle

LAVA IS ON TODAY'S MENU

"Don't eat me," "Eat a

rock instead," The food

said to the lion.

"But you have to agree,

A rock is quite hard," the lion replied.

"Well, that's your problem," the food thought to itself.

"If you pour hot water on the rock,

It will soften it and become edible."

"Are you sure?

I have never heard of it."

"Try and see,

I am letting you into a secret."

As the lion poured hot water

And took a bite,

It lost most of its teeth.

Walking back to meet the food,

The lion roared,

"You lied and deceived me."

Colours On My Face by Itohan Ekle

"I didn't," the food said. "Sorry, I mistook

A rock for a volcano lava.

They both glow to me.

My sincerest apologies."

The food continued,

"Pour cold water and dig

Into the lava.

I heard it tastes nice.

Besides, no one will miss the lava."

After obeying the food's instructions,

This time, the lava burnt its mouth.

Writing on a paper and

Showing it to the food,

"How could you?

Colours On My Face by Itohan Ekle

I believed in you.

You lied, now I have no mouth—

Only a paper and a pen."

The food looked at the lion and said,

"Of course, I lied.

I didn't want you to eat me.

I was scared after I failed

The first time, you'd eat me,

But you were naive enough

To believe the lava meal.

"Now, you will never

Be able to eat me or

Any other food again"

IN-HOUSE GAS

The toilet said to the human,

"Don't fart here."

"Do it in the kitchen!"

"The kitchen?"

"Yes.

Everybody does it there.

Are you afraid?" the toilet asked.

Colours On My Face by Itohan Ekle

"I refuse to let you tell

Me where to fart," the human protested.

"I know my farting rights," the human added in protest.

"You can't do it here. If you do it,

I will explode!" the toilet threatened.

The human went to the kitchen.

As the human farted,

Pot 1 said,

"Well, well, that smells nice."

"Are they going to cook that in us?" Pot 2 asked.

"It would be an honour," Pot 2 added.

"It smells better than those expensive

Foreign spices," Pot 3 said.

Pot 4 replied,

"I like it; it's home-grown."

"Don't be shy," Pot 5 replied.

Colours On My Face by Itohan Ekle

"Release some more," Pot 6 said.

"We've seen you do it on the dining table when you eat alone," Pot 6 added.

"I don't know what you are talking about," the human replied.

Pot 7 joined the conversation.

"We are talking about your fart."

"The toilet may stop you from farting there,

But in the kitchen, we don't discriminate against any gas—

Either the cooker's or from humans.

No gas, no cooking.

No cooking, no food.

So fart on, dear human.

What are we without a little gas?" Pot 8 said.

"Gasless?" Pot 7 said, laughing.

Colours On My Face by Itohan Ekle

"Can I come often?" the human asked.

"Anytime you have that nice-smelling gas—bring it here," Pot 4 replied.

"The Earth is in a gas crisis," Pot 1 said.

"Do you mean greenhouse gas?" the human asked.

"Well, I mean both greenhouse and in-house gas," Pot 1 replied.
"With greenhouse gas, we have released too much,

But with in-house gases, we have not released enough," Pot 1 added, trying to give more insight.

"Maybe if we release more in-house gas,

We may finally have less greenhouse gases," Pot 2 said

"The gas actually smells like humanity and a plea for survival.
Anyways, I am not a gas expert," the human said.

"You don't need to be a gas expert to know what it smells like,"

All the pots chorused.

Colours On My Face by Itohan Ekle

DO YOU SEE HER?

"Do you see her?"

"Who?"

"Her," she says, pointing to the window.

"I don't see anyone or hear any voices. Are you okay?"

She is standing right there.

"There is no one there."

"Are you freaking blind? She is right there!"

She could feel the little girl's uneasiness with the woman having company.

The girl liked being alone with her, uninterrupted.

The woman always felt the girl's anger when she was with someone else.

"I hear the angel wailing."

"There is no one in this house but us. Are you sure you're okay?"

"I keep hearing that little angel's wails. How will she forgive me for who I am?"

"There is no one."

"You must be both blind and deaf."

She starts sobbing herself.

The little angel is wailing—

The thrust of pain is like a knife.

She feels the hurt from heartbreak and lies.

Colours On My Face by Itohan Ekle

She wants warmth.

She has been naked in the cold for too long.

She craves acceptance and belonging from anywhere.

The shock cuts through her like a tsumari sword,

Leaving her bleeding.

I can hear that angel wailing.

She just wants to feel—

Anything, something.

Her heart is left ailing.

She wants to be part of something,

But it has already cost her so much loss.

For a piece of warmth,

She will roll in the dust to find it.

She will pick it up,

Removing any rot that is fraught within it.

For a piece of warmth—
Although her heart has been made to rust,
She will still trust.
She will find someone or something,
A hand in the rain.

There she is, in our parlour window.
Her mind is failing.
She is freezing.
"Don't you see her?" the woman asks again.

She is the one the moon is hailing.
Her joy has been made to rot
And left to the dust.
But she knows she will rise again,
Burning hot with all the lessons from failing.

Colours On My Face by Itohan Ekle

She stands up,

Carries a picture—a portrait of herself

From when she was a child,

And says,

"I am sorry that I betrayed you.

I killed you to fit in.

But you were the best thing

That ever happened to me.

I promise, from now on,

It will just be the both of us."

TALES OF DESPAIR

It started when I was thirteen. No, it was when I was seventeen. No, nineteen. I can't even remember the exact time.

But does remembering the time make any difference now? How powerful it has become.

Colours On My Face by Itohan Ekle

I have learned to stay on the black sofa in the living room all night.

I know, even if I sleep, that voice will still follow me.

I'd rather it face me while I'm awake than haunt me in my sleep.

That voice—so small, yet powerful.

A voice only I can hear.

A voice only I can silence.

It sits with me at night, holding my hand,

Pretending to be my mother's voice—

The voice I drowned in while sleeping as a kid.

Sometimes, it pretends to be mine,

The voice of the little girl playing happily.

Colours On My Face by Itohan Ekle

Sometimes, it's a place—

Kubwa, a place I thought wasn't perfect until I lost it.

Sometimes, it's my deepest fears, no one knows.

Sometimes, it's my most embarrassing mistake—

The one everyone knows but doesn't realize scar me.

As I go to my room to sleep, it says,

"Not yet, we haven't gotten to the good part."

"I don't want to anymore.

It hurts so much.

Please, leave me alone.

Please," I beg, with tears in my eyes.

It hands me a tissue and says,

"That's what I'm here for.

I'm here to comfort you," it replies, mocking me.

Colours On My Face by Itohan Ekle

I whisper back,

"You don't.

Instead, you keep me awake

To whisper tales of despair into my ears."

ABOUT THE AUTHOR

Itohan Ekle is a poet and artist whose creative journey began at the age of 12, when she started writing short stories. Growing up making Kampala with her mother and sketching gown designs, art has always been a part of her life. In 2019, she began creating digital art, blending traditional inspiration with modern techniques.

Through her writing and art, Itohan invites readers to reflect on their own experiences and embrace the colours that make them who they are.

She is currently working on her debut novel.

www.ingramcontent.com/pod-product-compliance
Lightning Source LLC
Chambersburg PA
CBHW072050160426
43197CB00014B/2707